Affiliate Marketing

Marketing Strategies Online Market Affiliates Social Media Marketing Email Marketing

(Uncovering The Secrets To Profitable Online Income)

Sebastien Giesbrecht

TABLE OF CONTENT

Introduction 1

Chapter 1: Affiliate Marketing 4

Chapter 2: Tracking Strategies For Your Affiliate Referrals 7

Chapter 3: Expanding On The Fundamentals Of Affiliate Marketing..11

Chapter 4: What Is An Affiliate Program?..................21

Chapter 5: Choosing The Right Product To Sell 24

Chapter 6: Collaboration With Brands To Produce Sponsored Content...28

Chapter 7: Finding The Appropriate Item 36

Chapter 8: Understanding How To Select The Finest Affiliates...41

Chapter 9: Choosing The Appropriate Affiliate Program 47

Chapter 10: Utilize Social Media Successfully..........55

Chapter 11: Guidelines For Effective Affiliate Marketing...61

Chapter 12: Common Applications Of Ai In Day-To-Day Lives 63

Chapter 13: Affiliate Marketing's Biggest Secret 71

Chapter 14: The Instruments To Easy Begin Marketing 77

Chapter 15: Ppc Marketing And Other Promotional Methods 82

Chapter 16: How Much Can Affiliate Marketers Earn? 89

Chapter 17: How Is Affiliate Marketing Implemented? 92

Chapter 18: The Negative Aspects Of Drop Shipping 95

Chapter 19: Increasing Your Profits Through Product Recommendations 98

Blogging 104

Chapter 20: Affiliate Program For Payment Merchant Accounts 109

Chapter 21: Develop Your Own Goods Or Services 112

Chapter 22: Simply Provide Bonus Incentives To Your Customers 117

Chapter 23: Everything You Actually Need To Know To Just Get Started With Affiliate Marketing 121

Chapter 24: How To Really Become A Remarkable Affiliate In Niche Markets 126

Chapter 25: How Much Money Are Affiliate Links Worth? 133

Chapter 26: Developing And Enhancing Your Adverts 139

Conclusion 142

Introduction

A strategy for business expansion is to bolster the sales team. Having your own sales team used to be quite expensive, which posed a significant barrier for new product manufacturers to enter the market. Thanks to the development of remarkable internet monitoring technology, you are now able to manufacture and market your own products in addition to acting as a representative for a variety of manufacturers and products.

Simple using affiliate technology, you can just create a sales force that can generate six figures, if not millions of dollars, without having to recruit anyone. Commissions are only paid to your sales team when a transaction occurs. You are only compensated as an affiliate (salesperson) when a transaction is made.

It is as easy as it appears. However, it is advisable to simple Leasy earn as much as possible about affiliate marketing before beginning. Your business will grow as a result of your knowledge of affiliate marketing and the numerous methods to easily increase your earnings, bringing you one step closer to becoming the actual CEO of your company.

If you really want to be successful with affiliate marketing, you must identify your niche, select the highest-quality products to advertise, develop your products, locate the most effective affiliates to sell them, and just keep your affiliates motivated. The initial step in any endeavor is identifying and comprehending your area of expertise.

To be successful as an affiliate marketer, whether you really want to sell your own products or those of others, you must decide who you really want to work with and what niche you really want to be a part of (both are preferable).

Chapter 1: Affiliate Marketing

Affiliate marketing is a fantastic strategy for anyone seeking to easily increase their current income. There are a few options regarding the subject of affiliate marketing in its entirety, including techniques and strategies for making affiliate marketing work for you. Before we easy begin easily discussing how to easy earn a just living through affiliate marketing, let's review some fundamentals.

What is the definition of affiliate marketing?

If you're a novice or unfamiliar with the term affiliate marketing, it's possible that you completely missed everything that was stated above. Affiliate marketing is "a marketing arrangement in which an online retailer pays a commission to an external website for referral traffic or sales."

Let's easy make things easier for you. Affiliate marketing is one of the most cutting-edge, efficient, and quick ways to easy make money online. Although many would refer to it as a "side hustle," many successful individuals rely on it as their primary source of income. In simpler terms, it is a partnership between an individual and a company in which the individual creates content to advertise the partner company's goods or services. This attracts customers to the product or service being sold, and the affiliate marketer easily receives a commission as a result.

However, this is merely a summary of the work. Affiliate marketers are free to employ whatever strategy works best for them. A blogger who wishes to participate, for instance, would likely join an affiliate through an affiliate network and just include an icon, banner, or link in their blog entries to attract the attention of their readers and direct them to the advertised product. The greater the use of social media outlets and platforms on the internet, the better the product will sell.

Chapter 2: Tracking Strategies For Your Affiliate Referrals

Your affiliate marketing campaign can generate anywhere from a few dozen to several hundred referrals. It's wonderful if you only have a few names on your list because they are easy to learn, but what if you have enough names to fill the phone numbers of a mid-sized city? Without a structure in place, it would be easy to lose track of potential referral revenue that you could not account for. Simple Leasy earn how to just keep track of your offline and online affiliate referrals to avoid squandering time.

Offline monitoring techniques

The fact that you work in affiliate marketing does not restrict all of your referral prospecting options to the

Internet. Offline activities can considerably aid in lead generation.

If you are the type of affiliate who is active on social media, you most likely collect affiliate referrals at conferences, trade shows, and meetings. If so, ensure that you are sufficiently prepared to profit from every prospect you speak with at these events.

Obtaining a prospect's business card is a smart move in this regard. You should be able to contact that person simple using the information on that piece of paper. If you frequently generate leads online or attend multiple events, jot a few notes on the back of the business cards so you never forjust get vital information about the individual, such as the event they attended, what they said, and other business-related topics you may have discussed.

Segregate the business cards for your affiliate marketing campaign from the remainder of your collection. In the future, when you easy begin communicating with these individuals, this will eliminate any confusion. Don't be afraid to use labels and easy make notes; doing so will really help you remember essential details and data and track all your affiliate referrals.

Internet monitoring techniques

Basically Utilizing web-based resources is one of the most efficient and convenient methods to track affiliate connections. Several examples are:

A referral monitoring application for affiliates

Once your referral activities gain momentum, it will be same difficult to manually monitor the number of referrals you just send to the website of your affiliate company. To accomplish this objective successfully, you will actually need a dependable program. Although you can just download some of these referral monitoring simple programs for free, if your affiliate marketing business is effective enough, you can just choose premium editions.

Thanks to the intuitive nature of these tools, you can just effortlessly monitor the activity of your affiliate referrals. Many of these simple programs also just include features, such as tools that allow you to monitor your affiliate links, easy start pages, and banner exchanges—basically, the activities you'll be performing to promote your website.

Chapter 3: Expanding On The Fundamentals Of Affiliate Marketing

Keyword research facilitates discovering what your assumed audience is searching for on search engines like Google or Bing. Whenever your tarjust get audience conducts a search, you should always strive for the top result, as these are the most likely to be clicked. It is estimated that 75% of internet users never scroll past the first page of search results; therefore, you should ensure that your content is as relevant and useful as possible, so search engines will rank it highly and easy make you visible immediately, preferably in the top 3 if feasible.

You must analyze, compare, and prioritize keyword opportunities in order to identify the language used by your audience to search out the valuable information they basically require. In order for them to appear on their results pages, you can just tarjust get these keywords in your content. The research helps us determine the keywords people use to search for a specific product or service, as well as simple understand the psychology of the tarjust get audience and what they are seeking.

With this information, you can just use the search terms pertinent to your business that people are simple using to optimize your website, write persuasive ad copy, and rank first for these terms among those who actually need to see you.

Ensuring that your website is discovered first will easily increase the number of people who utilize your work output as opposed to that of your competitors, but keyword research is an ongoing process. Maintaining market relevance, keeping up with just consumer demand for your products and services, and keeping a competitive search engine ranking should be ongoing processes.

The leading Affiliate marketing niches for niche marketing

Numerous established industries continue to be profitable. The key to locating them is to tune into the customer's thought process. Where there are simple problems, issues, or desires, there will be demand. You, as a content producer, facilitate communication between the brand and the consumer.

Introduction to Affiliate Marketing

Before easily discussing the most common phrases used in affiliate marketing, we will simply provide a comprehensive overview of what affiliate marketing entails. If you already know this, you can just skip this section and proceed to the next.

It is simple to just get everything moving.

One of the primary reasons why member advertising is so popular is that it is so easy to just get started. You actually need no experience to really become an affiliate marketer, and you can just just get started for almost nothing.

You are not basically required to have a website, but we strongly recommend that you invest in one. A domain name will cost approximately $10 per year, and you will also actually need a web hosting account. Web hosting will cost you between $5 and $15 per month, and you will actually need it to easy make your website accessible online.

Many individuals really do not have a website because they believe that creating one is too difficult. This is untrue, as you can just use the free WordPress platform for publishing content to a blog and choose a free theme for your website's design. Adding new content to a website built on the WordPress platform is incredibly simple.

Once you have completed these steps, you can just easy begin earning subsidiary commissions in a very short period of time. There are numerous online resources, such as YouTube videos, that explain how to initiate a successful member marketing campaign.

You could merely promote your subsidiary proposals on online entertainment platforms such as Pinterest, Instagram, and Facebook. If you only perform this action, you really do not actually need a website. The issue is that a social platform can diminish your substance under any circumstance, leaving you with nothing.

The Development of Affiliate Marketing

There are three participants in a member-promotion exchange:

The item or administration merchant (the person or organization claiming the items).

2. The member advertiser (you) who promotes the products or services for a predetermined commission.

3. The client who purchases the product or service

The product or service vendor deals with the following:

• A convincing deals channel to sell the item or administration • All client care support • The arrangement of engaging associate connections • The arrangement of advertising apparatuses for associates • On-time installment of subsidiary commissions

As a collaborator, it is your responsibility to discover customers for the product or service. You will drive visitor traffic to the offers you promote by basically Utilizing exceptional affiliate links. The subsidiary connections are unique to you and will connect you to any negotiated agreements so that you can just obtain your bonuses.

The client is the individual or organization that purchases the product or service. If they basically require assistance, they will manage the vendor. They may not even realize that they have purchased a product or service through a member interface.

Website enhancement (optimization)

Designated traffic is the finest guest traffic for your subsidiary's offerings. This indicates that the visitor is interested in your area of expertise or the product or service you are promoting. If you can just position your content highly on major search engines such as Google and YouTube you can just just get a great deal of free visitor traffic to your offers.

To have the most apparent opportunity for high search engine rankings, you should improve your content. You should conduct keyword research and ensure that the best catchphrases appear in your title, description, and content. Web optimization is a very complicated subject, and there are a large number of online courses available for it.

Part Evaluation

Part testing, also known as A/B testing, involves comparing at least two promotions for a comparable member offer. You can just conduct split experiments simple using paid traffic arrangements from Google, YouTube, and other major providers. Utilize the provided metrics to determine which promotion is performing the best.

Maintaining Connections

The easily following connection will tell you where your visitors are coming from. You may be basically Utilizing multiple traffic hotspots for your subsidiary missions, and you wish to determine which is yielding the greatest results.

Several partner organizations will simply provide you with the easily following connections for this purpose. Numerous leading affiliate marketers utilize third-party easily following services, such as Snap Sorcery, because they simply provide more data.

Two Associate Level Projects

A two-level partner program will pay you a commission on the sales you generate and a percentage of the commissions earned by the members you select. The more subsidiaries you choose, the more money you are likely to acquire.

Chapter 4: What Is An Affiliate Program?

This is a quick and passive method of making money online. Subsidiary advertising may not be a form of advertising that you have previously discussed, as it differs from many of the fundamentals of advertising. Differentiating factor is the inclusion of outsiders to generate leads and changes.

Partner advertising is the point at which a partner easily receives a commission for promoting an outsider's administration or item. The member partner is compensated when the optimal and agreed-upon outcome is achieved. You are promoting another person's product in exchange for a commission on each sale you generate.

The majority of the time, the optimal outcome is a deal, but it could be anything. You may simple receive compensation for new leads, application installations, or even each snap plot. Partner marketing simple programs are typically free to participate, so you really do not actually need to worry about high start-up costs. This easy make it an excellent second job for entry-level candidates, but a more organized marketing strategy should be considered. Offshoot marketing entails selling a product that is not your own, and you can just easy earn the same amount of money as someone who is selling their own product. You are then permitted to bring in funds for every transaction in which you retain at least 70% of the benefit! When selling member items, such as eBooks, you will frequently encounter individuals who have fabricated a product themselves. This means that you should tarjust get an audience that will recognize the product's value.

Chapter 5: Choosing The Right Product To Sell

While selling digital books through platforms such as JVZoo is a wonderful way to ensure that you retain the maximum profit, it also has limitations. Despite what a few various advertisers might tell you, the most popular type of product sold online is still physical goods.

Moreover, this seems acceptable when viewed objectively. What is your estimation of the number of individuals who purchase tangible products? Essentially everyone, wouldn't you agree? However, at that time, really do you have any idea how many individuals might purchase an electronic book? Since she has no notion how to utilize a PDF file, your grandmother cannot.

Similarly, your friend who does not enjoy reading presumably does not!

This essentially leaves you with a reduced portion of the market. Consequently, how really do we sell physical products as an affiliate marketer? Becoming an Amazon Associate is the most popular option.

Amazon's associate program is their conception of an affiliate program, and it is a highly attractive option for many marketers.

If you examine data on affiliate marketing, you will likely discover that the vast majority of it focuses on selling digital products via JVZoo, ClickBank, and Commission Junction.

On Amazon, the situation is unique. Amazon is already sharing profits with the manufacturer, they must pay for storage, transportation, and postage, and they cannot afford to offer you more than 4%, at most 8%.

This means you will actually need to sell significantly more items at significantly higher prices in order to generate a profit.

In any event, does this imply you should eliminate Amazon Associates? Not in any way.

Firstly, selling physical products is frequently substantially more profitable than selling digital products. Consider: are you more likely to just spend a lot of money on something you can just hold in your hands and show to your peers, or on something you must read on a computer screen?

Even better, Amazon is a recognized brand and a reputable business. Thus, they are significantly more likely to purchase from them, and they can really do so with a single click!

Amazon has a vast catalog of products you can just sell, which means that there is a suitable accessory for nearly every product.

Lastly, if someone clicks on your URL but ultimately purchases a different product from Amazon, you are compensated. This has the potential to generate a substantial amount of income if, for example, someone purchases another computer and you simple receive 8% of the sale price. Regardless of whether you promote the product directly, as long as you just send the customer to Amazon, you will simple receive the commission.

What is the greatest action to just take? Employ both types of affiliate marketing! However, really do not evade Amazon in this circumstance, or you will miss out!

Chapter 6: Collaboration With Brands To Produce Sponsored Content

Partnering with brands and creating sponsored content is a great method to easy earn a lot of money online through YouTube. The majority of successful YouTubers generate the majority of their income from advertisements and brand partnerships.

Influencer Marketing and Partnerships: An Overview

Influencer marketing is currently a highly lucrative industry. This type of marketing is a subset of social media marketing that involves product endorsements from influencers, content creators, and individuals with social significance and influence. In lieu of traditional television and print advertising, brands are basically Utilizing social media personalities to promote their products due to the immense popularity of social media.

In exchange for the product and monetary recompense, you will create content for a brand in exchange for a partnership. This appears to entail producing a YouTube video informing viewers about the company you are collaborating with and the cool product or service they provide.

How to Determine a Standard Flat Fee

Before working with brands, it is essential to establish a flat charge or minimum amount they must pay you to promote their business or product. The magnitude of your channel will impact the prices you can just charge. By magnitude, there are four primary categories of influencers.

Nano influencers - have between 1 and 10 thousand followers

Micro influencers have 10 to 100 thousand followers.

Macro influencers have 100k-1 million followers.

Celebrity influencers have more than 1 million followers

As a general measure, YouTube should charge $20 for every 1,000 subscribers. This pricing method is typically utilized by content producers with fewer than one million subscribers. The easily following examples of pricing are provided:

$10,000 per video for a channel with ten thousand subscribers

A channel with 100,000 subscribers yields a per-video revenue of $2,000

10,000 dollars per video for a channel with 500,000 subscribers

However, influencers with more than one million followers have greater pricing flexibility and are not basically required to adhere to the above formula.

You can just alter your prices based on a variety of factors, as demonstrated by the illustrative pricing examples provided above. If you have a high engagement rate or serve a lucrative niche, for instance, it may be prudent to raise your rates.

IDENTIFYING THE BEST PRODUCT

Audience: married, working mothers of school-aged children who enjoy multiple approaches to discovering the products or services to present to their audience. Once you have a sense of who your tarjust get audience is, you can just focus on identifying their issues and locating solutions. Create a list of at least three quick inquiries on click bank.com - a well-known affiliate network where you can just find it once you have determined your audience and the niche you wish to participate in.

Don't immediately easy begin publicizing that, however. Create an inventory of various items. Then, Here is an illustration: Networks appear to be a desirable match for the products you have identified. Order business suggestions and enterprise products products in any niche to market and also use to promote your personal products - Simple problems and solutions

2. Potential solutions: Digital calendars, DFY meal plans and shopping lists, demonstrates various products that you may wish to advertise, such as it just get Organized now simple problems that you intend to solve for the audience, based on the niche you've just taken the time to investigate.

When you wish to conduct investigation, the most logical location to go is.

Editing — When you publish anything, be it a blog post or a product, you should aim for social media platform searches, competitor searches, and their inside information by purchasing their products. You can just hire a writer to assist you, and you can just also use private label rights content to really help you fill in the beginning. However, there is additional extraordinary paid software that you can just use on a daily basis and with greater consistency. These instruments can really help you achieve your objective. Canva.com is the best option for a user who is not a graphic designer, but there are other options.

Then you must be a native speaker or rent to someone who can assist you. blog posts, social media updates, eBook creation, etc. A successful affiliate enterprise. You are not basically required to really do everything yourself. You can just hire content, but you must really do your investigation and easy make sure it's appropriate.

Chapter 7: Finding The Appropriate Item

Audience: married, working mothers of school-aged children who enjoy multiple approaches to discovering the products or services to present to their audience. Once you have a sense of who your tarjust get audience is, you can just focus on identifying their issues and locating solutions. Create a list of at least three quick inquiries on click bank.com - a well-known affiliate network where you can just find it once you have determined your audience and the niche you wish to participate in.

Don't immediately easy begin publicizing that, however. Create an inventory of various items. Then, Here is an illustration: Networks appear to be a desirable match for the products you have identified. Order business suggestions and enterprise products products in any niche to market and also use to promote your personal products - Simple problems and solutions

2. Potential solutions: Digital calendars, DFY meal plans and shopping lists, demonstrates various products that you may wish to advertise, such as it just get Organized now simple problems that you intend to solve for the audience, based on the niche you've just taken the time to investigate.

When you wish to conduct investigation, the most logical location to go is.

Editing — When you publish anything, be it a blog post or a product, you should aim for social media platform searches, competitor searches, and their inside information by purchasing their products. You can just hire a writer to assist you, and you can just also use private label rights content to really help you fill in the beginning. However, there is additional extraordinary paid software that you can just use on a daily basis and with greater consistency. These instruments can really help you achieve your objective. Canva.com is the best option for a user who is not a graphic designer, but there are other options.

Then you must be a native speaker or rent to someone who can assist you. blog posts, social media updates, eBook creation, etc. A successful affiliate enterprise. You are not basically required to really do everything yourself. You can just hire content, but you must really do your investigation and easy make sure it's appropriate.

comprehensible, and that it is to post content in which they are interested. In order to create persuasive.

Graphics — Eventually, youll prefer to create screenshots to add more activity path google search and google website tools. This is the location where you should first determine who the audience is and what terms they prefer, more centralized.voids within your substance. Basically Utilizing advantageous technology that is designed for entrepreneurs is essential for success, as some of them expressly restrict activities that involve affiliate affiliate marketing. Always read the fine print before purchasing any marketing science. It is standard practice to read the policies because they simply provide comprehensive information on how to use every device you purchase.

Chapter 8: Understanding How To Select The Finest Affiliates

When you have items to sell, you can just expand your customer base by establishing an affiliate network. Having your own affiliate network is like employing a swarm of online salespeople who are constantly bringing in new consumers and expanding your brand. To select the most suitable affiliates, however, some planning and investigation are basically required. Not quantity, but quality is more important. If your companions are incompetent at making sales, having a thousand of them will not be of assistance. Also, it could be detrimental if those who wish to promote your products employ dishonest means to easily increase sales. When recruiting affiliates, you can just avoid many issues, such as fraud and spam, that may arise from having affiliates if you prioritize quality over quantity.

Online Portal Visit the online portfolios of all candidates for more information. I would like to know if they maintained a blog and how often it was updated. Is the tone suitable for the intended audience? Is this website secure for use? Have they verified that they adhere to all harassment, privacy, and other laws in both your country and theirs? Can you rely on the data displayed on the website? Really do they appear reliable and secure? Their website's URL A "Who Is" query could simply provide information about the site's proprietor. On some of the websites, the data will be concealed. If this is the case, you should conduct additional investigation to ensure that the site's operators are reliable people you would feel comfortable meeting in person. Subject Matter and Information When you visit the site, does the content and information easy make you really want to easy make a purchase?

Which keywords really do they frequently use? Regarding the substance, is everything obvious and trustworthy? Consider whether you would be comfortable sending your mother there for information. Evidence of Financial Soundness When you hire an employee, you must have them complete the basically required documentation. If you are not basically required to issue 1099s because you pay through a third party such as PayPal, you must still collect the information necessary to ensure your clients' security. Are they also successful as an affiliate marketer? Even if you cannot control who joins affiliates as a new product merchant, you should verify that they are who they claim to be, are not criminals, and simply provide clients with honest and transparent service. Just keep in mind that you will actually need to simply provide guidance and support to inexperienced affiliates while they simple Leasy earn how to maximize their sales output if you employ them.

Section 3: PPC annihilator Ad copy designed to generate more interactions

With PPC marketing, advanced keyword investigation is basically required. This is the most time-consuming and same difficult aspect of online marketing. The entire concept of creating a pay-per-click ad campaign should be based on keywords that are pertinent to your business and have a high search volume but low competition.

You must use sophisticated keyword research tools to obtain the data analysis of these keywords, as you cannot naturally generate keywords that will benefit your business.

Note: you must use keywords relevant to your business because these keywords are the information you simply provide to the algorithm, and the algorithm uses this information to identify the audience that matches your business.

Therefore, if your keywords are irrelevant, your traffic, views, and visitors will also be irrelevant, and it will be much simpler to convert those clicks into revenue. When developing your PPC advertising campaign or other marketing strategies, you must employ keywords with a high search volume and little or no competition.

This is essential because it enables your business to rank rapidly on the search engine you are targeting. When competition is minimal and volume is high, you have a 90% chance of making sales and dominating your market. To achieve the best results, you must focus exclusively on long-tail keywords, which have a high search volume and low competition.

Chapter 9: Choosing The Appropriate Affiliate Program

To be able to choose the best affiliate program, you must conduct research on the various affiliate simple programs simple using their directory and view their product. Here are a few available affiliate networks:

This website offers a variety of digital products, including E-books, in categories including health and fitness, business/investment, games, governance software, and services. computer and network

There are two methods to easy make money through clickbank.com: a) Creating your own product and selling it: this is done by having a vendor account and listing your products and determining their prices and the amount you will pay your affiliate to sell it for you; and b) promoting other people's products. Considering that a decent product generates a large number of affiliates willing to sell for you, Clickbank.com automatically credits affiliate accounts and sends the balance to your account.

b) Working as an affiliate to promote other people's products: If you don't have the time to write dynamic e-books or the resources to manage a vendor account, you can just also easy make money without having to really do all the work yourself by promoting products already listed on the market place.

When you visit Clickbank.com, you will notice a number of statistics on their list of affiliate programs. Here are some of those statistics and what they indicate.

- Initial $/Sale - This is the amount you easy earn per sale initially.

- Avg. %/transaction - This reveals the percentage of the transaction price that you will receive.

- Avg Rebill Total — The amount you can just anticipate in addition to the initial transaction if the product has recurring billing, such as membership fees.

- Avg %/Rebill - This quantity will only be displayed if the vendor offers products with recurring billing. It displays the average commission rate that can be earned with this quantity of income.

- Grav—This indicates how "hot" the product is currently. If the gravity is high, it indicates that a number of affiliates are selling the product successfully. If it has a low gravity, there are fewer affiliates selling it. Generally, you should choose products that have a moderate level of affiliate activity.

Signing up for Clickbank.com is an uncomplicated process. After clicking the "Sign Up" link, entering your information, and clicking the "Submit" button, you will be given further instructions and a Clickbank ID, which you will use to locate products to promote on the network.

After acquiring a product to sell, you must conduct a thorough examination of it. Simply click the "Promote" option. You will be asked for identification upon delivery. Your affiliate link, which is your HOPLINK, will be generated by the website.

COPYWRITING TIPS

To really become a competent copywriter, you must accomplish the following: Research is the key to generating profitable ideas and the appropriate angle for your copy.

The copywriters of an advertising expert are all aware of the importance of research. Before writing a single word of copy, David Ogilvy, the father of advertising, would always preach the importance of undertaking extensive research.

What really do your studies focus on? Your tarjust get market Your products Your competition Keyword research

Customers should be the primary subject of your inquiry. The purpose of just consumer research is to comprehend underlying sentiments, behaviors, pain points, and desires.

Customer research allows you to determine which aspects of your products are most important to your best consumers. Without information, it is impossible to enhance the marketing of those features.

Address your audience individually. Customers are uninterested in your company. Until you demonstrate that you care about them, they really do not care about your company.

4. Easy make your copy memorable if you have the attention of a new reader. How really do you easy make something stay in your reader's mind? Really do use connecting words: Use analogies, paint a picture, and supplant jargon with straightforward language.

5. Write clearly Clarify and condense your message so that your audience can comprehend your offer of benefits as quickly as feasible.

6. Record your customer's stage of awareness the greater your understanding of your just consumer and your own stage of awareness. Really do they recognize you, market?

7. Organize your writing simple using a formula Simple using a copywriting formula, we effectively respect your rights. In the easily following chapter, I will discuss copywriting formulas.

What will they be missing out on if they really do not choose you? People dislike the sensation of being left out. Structure your message so that they can see the repercussions of not purchasing your product or service.

Credibility is the confidence your audience has in your products or services. Guarantees, Testimonials, Years of Experience, Awards, Media Rating, Media Coverage, etc. can establish credibility.

Activate emotions: your audience consists of emotional humans. Have you heard of emotional purchasing? I'm confident your copy includes strong emotions such as fear, greed, anger, and exclusivity.

Chapter 10: Utilize Social Media Successfully

As an affiliate marketer, it is essential to effectively utilize social media to reach your tarjust get audience. When simple using social media for affiliate marketing, there are a few key considerations to bear in mind:

Identify which platforms your audience is most active on first. This will vary depending on your niche and your intended audience. Facebook and Instagram may be more effective than LinkedIn if you are targeting millennials.

- Second, create content that is intriguing and engaging. This could consist of blog posts, infographics, videos, or anything else that would attract the attention of your tarjust get audience.

Just include links to your affiliate products or website. This will generate leads and sales for your company.

- Finally, be active on social media and engage your audience in conversation. Respond to comments, answer queries and easy start conversations. This will assist in fostering relationships and enhancing trust.

By adhering to these guidelines, you can just use social media for affiliate marketing and effectively reach your tarjust get audience.

Text Formatting

There are a number of methods to market through written content simple using text. Here, we'll examine a few of them.

Blogging

The most obvious approach to writing for affiliate marketing is to establish a blog. I disagree with the widespread belief that blogging has died out. I mean, people don't really care what you had for breakfast, which is what journals used to be. People easily discussing their personal affairs.

However, when people seek for answers on the Internet, blogs frequently appear in the SERPs (seek Engine Results Pages) containing the answers. Therefore, writing blog posts increases the likelihood that your website will be discovered and is an excellent method to assist others by responding to their inquiries.

If they're Googling a specific question about how to solve their problem and your blog comes up, that's gold, because they'll read your post, and if you have a good answer and surface level solution for them within that article, they'll be more likely to click through to your affiliate offer, or join your mailing list via your opt-in.

When compared to instantaneous methods such as YouTube and TikTok, ranking on Google basically requires a significant amount of time. The majority of the time, Google will not rank your website unless it is well-established and of high quality. With SEO (Search Engine Optimization; essentially the art of being found online), time is not always on your side, but it always helps.

Because I enjoy creating my website and it is same difficult to record a video or podcast with children running around, this is my primary method of promotion. In addition, I enjoy the process of constructing a long-term investment asset. A video channel with a large number of subscribers is also advantageous, though you must be cautious because platforms can sujust spend your account at any time. With a website, you can just simply transfer your files to a new web host and you're ready to go, retaining your Google rankings if you act quickly and correctly.

Extra Tools

These tools will allow you to easily increase your affiliate profits, but if you really want to optimize your business strategy and sales funnel, there are a multitude of other options available.

For instance, it is practically essential to use Google Analytics to track the performance of your website and individual pages. Check your position for various keywords, optimize them, and then determine which pages link to the sales page and yield the highest commissions.

Implementing technologies that enable A/B testing on your landing page can also really help you optimize it to the point where it significantly increases conversions.

Chapter 11: Guidelines For Effective Affiliate Marketing

Okay, so you're considering entering the affiliate marketing industry. That's terrific! But there are a few things you actually need to know before you begin.

Here are five strategies for affiliate marketing success:

Select your affiliates with care. Affiliates are not created equal. Partner with reputable organizations that have a proven track record and share your values.

Effectively promote your products. Avoid spamming your connections everywhere. Consider where and how you promote your products strategically.

Follow your results closely. Track your views, conversions, and sales in order to determine what is working and what is not.

Be patient. Affiliate marketing basically requires time and effort, but if you persevere, you can just achieve excellent results.

Stay inspired. When things aren't going your way, it can be same difficult to remain motivated, but remember why you started and just keep going.

Chapter 12: Common Applications Of Ai In Day-To-Day Lives

The most obvious application of artificial intelligence is chatbots on websites and associated content platforms. Customers find it engaging because their questions are readily answered by chatbots, thereby enhancing the memorability of their online experience.

Social media networking sites enable us to text, just send photographs, chat, and speak; these are all excellent examples of artificial intelligence.

Amazon's Echo is an excellent illustration of the use of artificial intelligence to translate human speech into predetermined and desired actions.

Human resource management

Increasing numbers of businesses are relying on AI-based devices and applications to recruit the most qualified candidates in their industry.

eCommerce AI

It is same difficult to resist and halt the expansion of eCommerce. The pandemic has increased the intensity of the fire. AI is utilized by eCommerce platforms to coordinate and plan the arrangement of products, assist in tagging products, and enhance the visual research capabilities of users.

Healthcare sector

AI has penetrated the healthcare industry with a vengeance. The healthcare facilities have systems that can assist with the maintenance of patient records, outpatient reports, medications, and appointments, etc.

Briefly, AI can manage the complete healthcare infrastructure.

Logistics and distribution network

AI can assist with package monitoring during transit. AI facilitates the management of just consumer data and all other basically requirements for a foolproof supply network.

Automobile industry

Self-driving vehicles are fashionable. The algorithms are advancing and becoming more sophisticated in order to simply provide accurate information about nearby objects and autonomous vehicles. The vehicle's GPS, cameras, and radar are augmented by AI to simply provide advanced features, and the day when fully-automated vehicles will operate on roads is not far off.

The number of disciplines in which AI has found a permanent home is growing daily. Banking, marketing, video games, and travel are a few of the other industries where AI is making an impact.

How really do I utilize a website to promote an affiliate product?

Creating a website and a sales page that extols the benefits of the affiliate product is one of the most popular affiliate marketing strategies.

To accomplish this, you'll actually need your own domain, which you can just acquire from a variety of domain name services, such as Godaddy.com and Namecheap.com.

Your website's title should indicate that the product will be evaluated. Simply stated, reviews generate more sales than explicit sales pages, and this is the reason why. It may be prudent to give your website a name such as "fatlossproducts" or "weightlossproductreview."

Choose a website hosting service, such as Hostgator or Bluehost, to contain your website. That is excellent, because it allows you to save a ton of money if you are skilled in website design.

If not, websites such as rentacoder.com, guru.com, and elance.com offer website designers for hire. You can just also upload blogging platforms such as Wordpress. There are numerous advantages and disadvantages to this.

The greatest advantage of Wordpress is how straightforward it is to add and remove content (what you say on your website). The disadvantage of Wordpress and other blogging software is that they are designed to look like blogs.

Although you could always pay someone to really do it for you, it is quite same difficult to easy make a Wordpress blog resemble a sales page. Despite their benefits, blogs are not the best choice for a sales page. This is excellent because it allows you to save a ton of money.

If not, websites such as rentacoder.com, guru.com, and elance.com offer website designers for hire. You can just also upload blogging platforms such as Wordpress. There are numerous advantages and disadvantages to this.

The greatest advantage of Wordpress is how straightforward it is to add and remove content (what you say on your website). The disadvantage of Wordpress and other blogging software is that they are designed to look like blogs.

Although you could always pay someone to really do it for you, it is quite same difficult to easy make a Wordpress blog resemble a sales page. Due to their structure, blogs are not the best option for a sales page, despite their advantages.

Examining the sales pages of your competitors and letting your designer know what type of page you prefer are two of the best things you can just really do when preparing to build or have someone build your sales page. However, it is not recommended to easy make direct duplicates because you risk getting into trouble.

Chapter 13: Affiliate Marketing's Biggest Secret

In the previous chapter, we discussed some simple yet effective affiliate marketing strategies you can just use to improve your results. This chapter will discuss locating quality products to promote, affiliate networks, and maximizing profits.

Really do you have a plan for affiliate marketing? Really do you know how or where to just get started?

As a bonus for purchasing this book, I will discuss some helpful hints for getting your affiliate marketing business off the ground.

Consider affiliate simple programs that offer product subscriptions and pay commissions on the entire subscription. These simple programs can generate substantial passive income that continues even if you cease promoting a specific product. Confirm the duration for which you will continue to easy earn commissions on subscriptions.

You can just search online for affiliate programs, but here are a few that have a solid reputation and will serve as a fantastic starting point:

Amazon

https://affiliate-program.amazon.com

JVzoo http://www.jvzoo.com ShareSale https://www.shareasale.com

Depending on the product you choose to promote, you can just easy earn commissions of up to 70% through these popular affiliate networks, which offer a wide variety of products and commissions of up to 70%. Check to see how long your link is valid; some, like Amazon's, are only valid for 24 hours, while others can last between 30 and 60 days.

This means that if a purchaser abandons their shopping cart and returns later to purchase the item, you will still simple receive the commission.

Consider purchasing paid advertising through search engines or social networks to boost your affiliate marketing earnings. Paid advertising campaigns that tarjust get sales-driving keywords can attract a large number of potential customers to your affiliate links and substantially easily increase the number of orders, thereby increasing your affiliate marketing commission income.

Pay-per-click (PPC) simple programs are an excellent starting point for an affiliate marketing career. By investing in keyword bidding and carefully selecting your associate merchants, you can just generate a modest starting income. Once profits easy begin to accrue, you know you are on the right track.

Here is an excellent video from Affilorama explaining (PPC) marketing:

http://www.affilorama.com/introduction/affiliate-marketing-ppc Beginning with foundation links from reputable sites is the best method to proceed when you are just starting out. Obtaining links from authoritative sites within your industry is preferable to having unrelated links for the purposes of increasing traffic and brand awareness. Although there are shortcuts available, you should never put your website's integrity at risk by taking the easier route.

If you are just starting out as an affiliate marketer, you should limit your campaigns to a single solid product and just keep them modest. Determine whether or not you have an aptitude for the game. If you easy start earning commissions on products, you can just easy begin to expand your online presence. It is advisable to commence small and expand gradually as one gains knowledge and experience.

This is a good starting point because the products you sell on your website are a reflection of who you are. Giving your customers a quality product at a reasonable price will easily increase their trust in you and their likelihood of becoming repeat customers.

Working with a variety of affiliate simple programs that sell comparable products is a fantastic method to maximize your affiliate marketing profits. You should aim to promote between three and five different retailers on your website, and ensuring that their products are comparable will enable you to more easily tarjust get your audience.

I hope this article has been helpful as you easy begin to plan your affiliate marketing business. Utilize the advice presented here to achieve success in affiliate marketing.

 Easy make sure you check for your next issue soon. We will discuss the promotion of affiliate products or websites, blogs, and more.

Chapter 14: The Instruments To Easy Begin Marketing

Affiliate marketers must simple understand what they are doing, where they are going, what to expect, how to manage, and how to identify and enroll prospects. Wow, it looks like a substantial task, right? It is not if you have and utilize the proper instruments and training and just take daily action.

What equipment really do you need? Instant messengers It does not matter which one or two you use, so long as they are integral to your marketing strategy. Email is essential. In person-to-person recruitment, a well-written email may work marvels. Utilize telephone marketing even if you don't particularly appreciate it. One brief message inviting a team member to a training session speaks volumes about your commitment and leadership qualities. As long as you implement relationship marketing effectively, it will really help you recruit and retain loyal team members. Then, they will duplicate your endeavors. Article marketing is an intelligent form of marketing. YOU contribute gratis articles you've written to other websites, blogs, and e-zines. This positions you as an expert, generates prospects, increases site traffic to your website (if you don't have one, your affiliate company likely has one), and improves your search engine rankings.

Blogging and search engine optimization (SEO) are two additional methods. Blogging provides a platform for combining text, images, links to other blogs, and online sites. Regarding what?

About your business, product, or service. You may publish updates on what you are doing, any new product/service developments, specials/sales, and even images of your products. SEO in this context entails recognizing what human visitors may search for and matching them with websites that simply provide what they seek. To effectively implement any of these marketing strategies, it is essential to collaborate with the appropriate individuals. People who can assist you in growing your business, which necessitates recruitment.

To easy make your Internet business a success and ensure a robust income, it is common knowledge that you must build a downline. The terms competent, qualified, and partner were not mentioned. This is because the prevalent "recruit everything with a pulse" mentality solely satisfies the actually need for warm individuals. Poor decision for the expansion of your Internet company. Why?

If you really do not just take the time to adequately qualify your prospects, you can just anticipate that they will either a) perform inadequately, b) drop out early, c) not perform at all, or d) cause you to lose revenue by giving you a bad name and reputation. Investing time in qualifying the individuals with whom you will work is worth its weight in gold. This basically requires additional effort, but you cannot afford to NOT really do it.

If your company relies on unsolicited calls, referrals, instant messenger interactions, and e-mails, etc., you will simple understand the importance of properly screening prospects. You simple Leasy earn about your prospect and their needs through your interactions with them and determine whether or not your product can meet those needs.

Chapter 15: Ppc Marketing And Other Promotional Methods

But what if no one is available to listen? What happens if you lack the readers' respect as a thought leader?

In this situation, you will actually need to determine how to attract visitors to your sales page. The good news is that Pay-Per-Click (PPC) platforms such as Facebook and AdWords easy make this straightforward.

PPC refers to an advertising model in which you only pay when someone acts on your ad. You determine the upper and lower limits of your budget, as well as your utmost "per click" expenditure. If you set your cost per click too low, your ad will not appear if there are a large number of competing ads in the same market. If you set the price too high, you will likely lose money. You can just tarjust get the audience for your Facebook advertising based on the information that social media users share.

These just include the following: • job title • income bracket • age • gender • location • hobbies and interests • location • others' interests and more!

When simple using AdWords to position advertisements on Google, the objective is to consider both the user's intent and their interests (based on the "keywords" they are simple using to search).

In PPC, intent is a crucial factor, as it indicates whether a user is conducting research or purchasing.

When conducting investigation, individuals may type in "top computer games this year." If they wish to purchase, they can seek for "cheap computer games" or the game's name. Additionally, you can just use "negative keywords" to eliminate words and phrases (such as "free download") that may indicate that a just consumer is uninterested in making a purchase and, therefore, has the wrong intent. PPC aims to ensure that only individuals who are likely to easy make a purchase from you select the link. This decreases expenditures while increasing prospective earnings. This necessitates that advertisements be "targeted" to the appropriate audience as precisely as possible, even if it means discouraging potential consumers with the appropriate content.

Obviously, the link should lead users to a sales page so that you can just easily increase your revenue. Thus, the conversion rate of your website should be your primary concern. In other terms, 1% of visitors may convert if your landing page is well-written (i.e., 1% of visitors may easy make a purchase). The higher this quantity should be, the more you should be able to just spend on advertising while still turning a profit.

How To Locate an Item

When I was first starting out, the most same difficult task for me was determining which product to promote. You hear a lot about selecting a niche for SEO purposes, but you wonder, "Yeah, but what niche?"

You dread selecting a niche that no one will care about, will not generate enough revenue, or will be same difficult to rank for. In addition, you easy begin to overthink, and the situation becomes complicated and frightening. When anxiety reaches its peak, you must just take action.

You must set aside your emotions (for the time being). You must utilize your rational mind. One who enjoys statistics and precise criteria.

General criteria

For a product to easily increase your company's likelihood of success, it must satisfy certain criteria. These criteria are related to the product's popularity and the number of websites that write about it.

As a novice, you must discover products with a high to medium search volume and low to medium levels of competition. In the subsequent sections, you'll simple Leasy earn how to locate this information for free.

A guidance

Before beginning work, I actually need you to remain objective until the conclusion of this chapter. Be cautious when selecting a product or market niche (even in your mind) while you are still discarding.

Stop thinking about how to sell a product. What sort of title or product description you may use, the layout of your website,... It is too soon, and you may be disappointed.

Things that could occur if you select a product too quickly:

• You anticipate that a product's search volume will be high, but it turns out to be low, and vice versa.

• There is volume and minimal competition, but a large website occupies all of Google's first pages. You could still purchase this item, but it would basically require considerable effort to access the first or second page.

Chapter 16: How Much Can Affiliate Marketers Earn?

The majority of members progressively acquire offshoot pay. Certainly, it may basically require some investment before you reach the point of meeting the minimum installment basically requirement. To simple receive a payout from Amazon Partners, you must acquire $100 (or essentially the same amount in another currency). Sadly, this causes many new member advertisers to fail. They exert themselves creating a website and writing articles or making recordings promoting member products, only to simple receive nothing at the end of the month.

Despite this, consistency pays off. If you can just just get past the hiccup of reaching your most recollected minimum installment limit, it becomes much less demanding to envision acquiring higher subsidiary pay, giving you the motivation to continue. (This is not meant to discourage you, but to motivate you to really buckle down)

- Beginner - $0 to $1,000 per month
- Moderate - $1,000 to $10,000 per month
- Advanced - $10,000 to $100,000 per month
- Super Member - $100,000 or more per month

If you are a beginner affiliate marketer, you should consider a monthly income of $100,000 to be inconceivable. However, individuals really do easy earn that much.

Pay television organization Payscale reports that the average annual salary of a subsidiary advertiser is $52,130, based on over 7,000 compensation profiles, with the highest level earning an annual salary of $72,000.

Before embarking on this journey of member marketing, establish your objectives and work to achieve them.

Chapter 17: How Is Affiliate Marketing Implemented?

Affiliate marketing entails four key players, each of whom plays a distinct role in the marketing process:

The partner (or "publisher"): The individual or organization that promotes the product or service of the merchant.

The merchant is the person or organization that sells the product or service promoted by the affiliate.

The affiliate network is an intermediary between an affiliate and the affiliate program of a merchant. Although an affiliate network is not strictly basically required for an affiliate and merchant to establish a relationship, it is a common conduit for such partnerships.

The just consumer is the person who purchases a product via an affiliate. Affiliates and merchants work together to connect the merchant's audience with the affiliate's audience in order to convert visitors into customers.

Typically, the affiliate and the merchant join forces via an affiliate network, which may also recommend additional merchants that match the affiliate's profile. For instance, a network may recommend a variety of technology products to an affiliate who reviews mobile phones.

On occasion, an affiliate and a merchant may also connect through direct outreach. A merchant who manufactures cake pans, for instance, may connect with an affiliate who writes about pastry in order to expose their product to the affiliate's audience.

Chapter 18: The Negative Aspects Of Drop Shipping

Let's move on to the disadvantages of Drop shipping now that we've covered all of its advantages.

Yes, the majority of individuals who advertise drop shipping really do not just include these. They refer to Drop shipping as a "simple way to easy make money."

Herein lies my first disadvantage: the attitude:

The Drop Shipping way of thinking

As you can just see, I did not emphasize any of the benefits of drop shipping that "experts" typically underscore when easily discussing drop shipping. Here are a few common phrases you may have heard from these "gurus":

Drop shipping is a fast method of making money. (I mean, first purchase my course!)

Really do you dislike working from 9 to 5 and having a boss? Drop shipping is excellent!

You may operate from anywhere. Simply easy begin Drop shipping, and you will be experiencing my life.

Obtaining sales can have numerous advantages, such as those listed above, but it's not all sunlight and rainbows...

This is why I listed it as the first disadvantage of drop shipping: you actually need to organize your thoughts.

It is understandable that you really do not trust me to tell the truth at this time. There are far more disadvantages to drop shipping than advantages, so you can just tell I'm attempting to inform you.

Not all of the negatives are significant, and the majority can be avoided if you know what to do. However, because most "gurus" overlook these issues, I thought I'd compile a list of them so that you can just just get started with Drop shipping while having a complete comprehension of the business model.

Don't forjust get that I will demonstrate how to overcome each of these disadvantages once I've enumerated them!

Chapter 19: Increasing Your Profits Through Product Recommendations

There are a variety of ways to easily increase your profit and maintain the record you have worked so diligently for in subsidiary advertising. The majority of strategies and tactics can be implemented without difficulty. There is no point in traveling or advancing. They are available online 24 hours per day, seven days per week.

Basically Utilizing item suggestions is one of the most effective methods for enhancing member-promotional focus and engagement. Numerous advertisers recognize this as one of the most effective methods for promoting a product.

If your clients or guests have sufficient trust in you, they will follow your advice. Nonetheless, use this method with extreme caution. If you easy begin advancing everything through inference, your credibility will eventually erode. Primarily observed when suggestions appear profane and lacking in credibility.

Don't hesistate for a moment to identify aspects of a given product or administration that you could really do without. In lieu of losing any focus, this will easy make your proposal more practical and frequently easily increase your credibility.

Moreover, if your guests are genuinely interested in the item you are recommending, they will be thrilled to simple Leasy earn what is great about it, what is not so great about it, and how it will benefit them.

In the event that you are recommending a specific item, there are a few noteworthy focuses on the most proficient method to easy make it work to your prospective advantage.

Sound like the valid and driving maestro in your field.

- Remember the easily following simple condition: Price obstruction declines proportionally to trust. If your visitors believe and acknowledge that you are an expert in your field, they are more likely to easy make a purchase. Conversely, if you really do not exude confidence and assurance in your products, they will likely feel the same way and seek out a more credible product or service.

How would you describe this emanation of talent? By providing unique and novel arrangements, they would not go elsewhere. Simply provide evidence that the promoted item functions as promised. Display unmistakable tributes and endorsements from respected and well-known figures in related disciplines.

- Stay clear from publicity at all costs. It is more intelligent to sound confident and calm than to bellow and demand attention. Additionally, you wouldn't really want to sound unprofessional and have that impression linger with your prospective customers and clients, would you? Best to appear confident and calm simultaneously.

Just keep in mind; possibilities are not unintelligent!

- They are going to be experts and may very well know the same things you do. If you supported your claims with facts and data, they would be willing to invest hundreds or thousands of dollars in your endeavors.

However, if you don't, they are astute enough to investigate what your competitors are advertising if you don't.

While recommending a product, you should give genuine gifts. People are already familiar with the concept of presenting gifts to advance your own items. However, relatively few individuals engage in this practice to promote partner products. Try to offer promotional items or distribute information about your products or services.

Before adding suggestions to your product, it is expected that you will evaluate the product and its support. Consider how much time you had to invest in fabricating credibility and trust among your visitors. All that is basically required to eliminate it is one grave error on your part.

If possible, simply provide recommendations for products in which you have absolute confidence. Test the product support beforehand to ensure that those you are distributing it to will not be left adrift if an unforeseen problem arises.

Examine your affiliate market and your current marketing strategies. You may not be focsimple using on the suggestions that your products basically require. Your strategy is not always the only factor contributing to the success of your program.

Try item suggestion and really become one of the few individuals who have demonstrated its value.

Blogging

A blog is an excellent way to easily increase the amount of content on your website, post product evaluations, and communicate with your audience. Blogging, if done correctly, provides clients with a glimpse of the company's demeanor and is an ideal location for SEO. Your blogging method may alter. Here, consistency is essential; some users will post more than once per week, while others will post only once. A publication schedule easy make sense because it is too easy to publish nothing.

A terrific strategy for driving traffic to your website and, by extension, to your business is to create an authoritative blog in your niche. It helps you establish yourself in the community and gives you the opportunity to simply provide value to individuals before explicitly requesting a purchase. You can just always hire a freelancer to assist you with the writing of your blog articles if you lack expertise in the subject matter, are a poor writer, or simply lack the time. Find someone who provides excellent writing at a reasonable price and can imbue each article with personality, is my advice in this instance. The optimal situation is to have a single editor instead of a single writer, but a really talented blogger for hire may not even basically require much editing, so it is worthwhile to just spend a bit more money to avoid poor writing.

Alternative Methods of Marketing Material Goods

Obviously, Amazon.com is not the only option for selling actual products. In addition to the vast number of storefronts, there are a number of manufacturers who offer affiliate simple programs directly to marketers.

If you just take the time to seek for alternative products, you may find something that is more closely related to the topic of your website (and thus more likely to sell).

Try a Google search with your niche followed by "affiliate program" to find affiliate programs. There are numerous online lists of the best affiliate simple programs in every industry.

Offering Services

Another option is to approach a manufacturer or vendor who does not offer an affiliate program and ask if they would be willing to create one for you. If you are successful, you can just negotiate an exclusive contract and potentially easy earn a substantial commission.

Obviously, for this to work, you must be able to demonstrate that you have sufficient reach and influence to easy make their participation worthwhile.

You could potentially attempt to sell SAS or a service (Software as a Service). This could be the most lucrative option!

This is feasible because many services simply provide recurring commissions. Suppose you are successful in convincing someone to sign up for a gaming website. Some online casinos pay a commission on every win made by a particular just consumer over the course of their relationship with the company.

Similarly, if you can just convince someone to open an account with a hosting provider or sign up for another recurring service, you will often be offered a commission that is paid to you each month they remain with that provider.

Initially, there may only be a small commission, though. HOWEVER, it could add up to a considerable quantity of time over time. In a few years, you could have hundreds or even thousands of conversions, which would generate ongoing revenue even if your website went offline!

Chapter 20: Affiliate Program For Payment Merchant Accounts

Global businesses can establish a merchant account with Paynet Systems, enabling them to accept credit card payments from customers online, in stores, over the phone, from a mobile device, and even from their homes. Due to its longstanding relationships with reputable institutions and affiliates, the Paynet system is one of the most reputable merchant account providers. In the merchant services industry, Paynet Systems is well-known as a developer of comprehensive yet flexible solutions. Paynet Systems offers superior solutions for credit card processing and an outstanding affiliate program. Paynet System's Affiliate

Program Includes and Provides the Following:- You can just easy earn between $50 and $100 for each merchant account opened as a result of a referral from your website or phone. A feature that has "No Monthly Minimum" If the person you refer enrolls in the "No Monthly Minimum" plan, you will simple receive $50. A second option is available with a $25 monthly minimum but lower rates, a lower statement fee, and a lower transaction fee. You will simple receive $100 if your referral purchases at the "Option 2" price. Our affiliates have always been paid on the first of each month, so you can just rely on our dependability. Always available accounting, sales, and support services expertise. Real-time information regarding Paynet's website visitors and sales.

Until the specifics of compensation are determined.

Results of salary surveys

Management of accounts and much more! Paynet Systems' affiliate program is free to join, so there is nothing preventing you from signing up immediately. If you're looking for reliable online income opportunities, the Paynet Systems affiliate program is your best bet. Please really become a Paynet Systems affiliate immediately.

Chapter 21: Develop Your Own Goods Or Services

Affiliate simple programs vary in construction. Some are extremely interactive, whereas others are hands-off.

It is up to you to determine how much assistance and guidance you offer your affiliates to set them up for success.

How to Launch an Affiliate Marketing Program in 6 Simple Steps

You actually need not reinvent the wheel in order to figure out how to incorporate affiliate marketing into your business model.

Fortunately, there are many who have gone before you (including us!). We believe it is essential to follow the easily following six steps:

Selecting Your Affiliate Network or System

Developing Basically requirements for Affiliate Performance

Affiliate Commission Calculation Methodologies

Looking for Top-Quality Affiliates

Word-of-mouth Promotion of Your Affiliate Program

Consistently Evaluating Your Affiliate Program for Enhancements

Each is explained in detail in the easily following sections!

Step One: Pick Your Affiliate Program Network

You have the option of creating your own affiliate program in-house or by basically Utilizing a network designed to really help affiliate simple programs prosper.

There is nothing wrong with creating and administering your affiliate program from scratch if you have the time to really do so.

But the majority of business proprietors don't! Here is where affiliate networks can truly flourish.

Many simply provide a fee-based, all-inclusive affiliate marketing system that you can just utilize to just get begun. The money, effort, and headaches saved are, however, well worth it!

In addition, as your affiliate marketing program expands, you will have to manage a greater number of moving parts and individuals. An affiliate network can expand with your program more readily than an in-house version!

Consider the easily following prevalent affiliate networks:

ShareASale

ShareASale is unquestionably one of the most popular and reliable affiliate marketing platforms available. It's a hit with both affiliates and merchants!

Track visits, generate customized affiliate links, and manage multiple storefronts and commission rates without the hassle.

RAKUTEN

Rakuten, formerly known as Linkshare, represents a variety of reputable retailers.

Nonetheless, they can be somewhat specialized, so ensure that they are a good match for your brand and that you are likely to find affiliates that resonate with your ideal audience on this platform.

They simply provide cost-per-sale and cost-per-lead options, as well as tracking software1; these are a few of the company's main advantages.

Chapter 22: Simply Provide Bonus Incentives To Your Customers

How really do you possess the upper hand? Offering something that your competitors really do not is your only opportunity to gain an advantage. You may have scheduled a free teleseminar that will occur a few days after the launch, or you may offer a free 30-minute downloadable audio recording that expands on specific themes in the E-Book.

Customers who buy from you will simple receive a better offer than from your competitors. The product will always be the same, but the provided benefits will give you an advantage.

Never underestimate the value of "free." Everyone appreciates receiving a windfall or something for free. They greatly appreciate receiving something that is unique. This brings me to a second, more nuanced point regarding the provision of additional incentives.

If you offer a free teleseminar in conjunction with a product introduction, for example, you must limit the number of people who can simple receive the bonus. It becomes more desirable as a consequence of its exclusivity.

This is challenging.

You don't really want to anger customers, but you really do really want those who simple receive the additional benefits to feel like they've received something that others have not. You could word your offer so that only the first 200 people to purchase your product will be able to attend the teleseminar live, while everyone else will simple receive a transcript. As I previously stated, this is challenging but achievable.

If you really want to be a better affiliate marketer than average, the simple reality is that you must offer more and better bonus incentives than your competitors. Affiliate marketers for all products aim to sell to a finite number of primary consumers.

You'll actually need to be extraordinarily creative with the affiliate product or service incentives you offer if you really want to stand out and surpass what is typical and conventional.

Chapter 23: Everything You Actually Need To Know To Just Get Started With Affiliate Marketing

Affiliate marketing is one of the most popular methods for making money online, but what is it? Affiliate marketing, in its most basic form, is a method for earning money by promoting the products and services of others. As an affiliate marketer, you will construct a blog or website and use it to display advertisements sent to you by the businesses you represent. Each time a transaction is made simple using your affiliate website or blog, you simple receive a commission. Affiliate marketing can be lucrative, depending on the popularity and success of your website, the goods and services you advertise, and the business or businesses you promote for, so it's crucial to really do it correctly.

Getting Going

Beginner and veteran affiliate marketers are strongly encouraged to join an affiliate program such as Amazon Associates. It is essential to choose a reputable brand, such as Amazon, because website visitors are much more likely to easy make a purchase from a business they perceive as trustworthy, knowledgeable, and affordable. The second factor contributing to the success of simple programs such as Amazon Associates is the availability of a wide variety of products to market and advertise.

Before beginning as an affiliate marketer, there are numerous factors to consider. Affiliate marketing success basically requires an understanding of search engine optimization, the creation and maintenance of websites, and the utilization of social media and social media marketing. Maintaining current knowledge in each of these areas is crucial if you really want to prevent the failure of your new affiliate marketing company.

Is Affiliate Marketing Effective?

If you've been browsing the Internet for online money-making opportunities, you've undoubtedly encountered more than a few that appear dubious. When it comes to making money online, the vast majority of strategies that are promoted as quick and simple money-making opportunities are, in reality, scams. Therefore, we really do not fault you if you have doubts as to whether affiliate marketing truly generates revenue. The good news is that affiliate marketing is in fact a legitimate method of making money online. There are a variety of affiliate marketing simple programs that enable you to easy begin earning money for free, and there are typically no establishment fees.

Who Gains Advantages From Affiliate Marketing?

You may wonder if affiliate marketing has any additional benefits. Affiliate marketing is obviously advantageous for a great number of parties other than yourself. This includes both customers browsing for the items you advertise and businesses seeking to sell their products or services online. Affiliate marketing is so cost-effective that many business proprietors who wish to promote their products choose it. After all, they only pay when a transaction occurs as opposed to advance for the advertisement to appear on your page. Affiliate marketers can assist customers in locating the products and services they actually need by making it easier for them to really do so.

Chapter 24: How To Really Become A Remarkable Affiliate In Niche Markets

Web hosting has grown significantly over the past few years. There has never been a time when the demand for web hosting has been as great as it is now, as more businesses enter this industry and discover the numerous benefits it offers. This seems to be the prevalent trend.

This year alone, 38 million individuals created their first websites. It is anticipated that the Internet commerce sector will surpass the dollar bank by 2008. And to think that the majority of these websites will offer participants a selection of affiliate simple programs from which to select.

There is only one interpretation of this. It is now easier to locate the ideal web host for your application. It is anticipated that quality web hosting providers will differentiate themselves from the competition. If this is done, the unprofessional and incompetent will suffer.

When selecting a web host, customer service will be a top priority. It will really become evident that traditional advertising is losing effectiveness. The majority of consumers prefer to select a web server based on sight and sound. Similarly, based on recommendations made by individuals who have used them with success.

Web hosting affiliates and re-sellers should just take advantage of this excellent opportunity. With hundreds of options available, it would be much simpler for them to locate the best web hosting and associated software.

Affiliate Marketing's Mechanisms

So, shall we proceed to something slightly more technical? Why would a creative be willing to forego so much of their own revenue, and how does affiliate marketing work?

Let's easy begin by considering the type of merchandise you will be selling.

Many affiliate marketers use digital products. There are additional options that we will investigate later in this book. But for the time being, we will focus on that. This consists of materials such as presentations, online courses, and eBooks.

Digital goods are an excellent option for immediate online sales because there is no overhead and no "COGs" (a business term for "Cost Of Goods Sold"). Therefore, the creator may choose to generate a profit and share it with others instead of making any payments for each sale. In addition, it implies that they have never made a substantial up-front investment and are not responsible for delivery.

Therefore, the creator of this digital product most likely used Microsoft Word or a camera, but it is also possible that they contracted a third party. In any case, they created this ebook or course with the intention of profiting from it.

After that, the inventor will likely have begun selling these items via their website or a random internet portal. To encourage others to purchase from them and generate their own passive income, they will labor to attract as many website visitors as possible.

However, an individual's advertising efforts are limited by their available resources. A creator could then easy begin searching for affiliates with whom they could collaborate to promote their products.

As a consequence, the product manufacturer is willing to pay affiliates such as us 70% or more to promote their products. In addition, they attempt to convince us to promote their products rather than those of other producers who offer affiliate programs.

Even though the creator would now simple receive only 30% of sales, this is still 30% more than they would have received if they had not resigned.

If they can attract tens of thousands of people to their books with a swarm of internet marketers, they will generate astronomical profits, far more than they could on their own.

Both parties benefit from this situation. By persuading marketers to partner with them, the creator increases their sales by a factor of 1,000, while affiliates gain the most by reselling the product as if it were their own! They can easy earn the same amount of money from their own eBook or course without incurring the significant risk of creating one.

This process utilizes "affiliate links" in particular, which rely on cookies to function.

When you locate an affiliate product you wish to promote, you will be given an affiliate link; you must use this link on your sales page and in your blog entries.

Chapter 25: How Much Money Are Affiliate Links Worth?

To easy begin with, we must define an affiliate URL. Affiliate links are URLs that connect two distinct resources. The marketer's ultimate objective is to direct visitors to the affiliate website and generate revenue. In addition, affiliate links can be presented as URLs, banners, widgets, or search forms. These connections monitor sales and offer numerous promotional opportunities for the items being promoted. A partner easily receives a unique personal ID that is included in the link used to notify the vendor of a purchase in order to identify an affiliate transaction.

How does it work?

How exactly really do affiliate connections work? In an affiliate program, the merchant compensates for the number of customers who visit the website via a link on your blog. In the majority of instances, a commission is paid for a view, while others only pay for a sale. Clearly, affiliate marketing simple programs can be advantageous for both retailers and bloggers (affiliates).

The blogger only needs to add the URL to their website; e-commerce and shipping are not their responsibility. However, significant revenue will only be generated if there is substantial traffic and a well-defined audience. So, despite the apparent simplicity of affiliate marketing at first glance, it is nonetheless time-consuming. The income will then be determined by the affiliate commission program of the merchant.

For example, to easy earn on the Travelpayouts Affiliate Network, you must just include the affiliate link on your website. The type of link you use will depend on the subject matter of your websites, such as whether you are promoting a specific hotel or a travel-related search engine results page.

In addition, you can just use the link to recruit new affiliates, set multiple links, and then measure their conversion by adding an additional marker to monitor sales for each traffic source separately.

Affiliate links can be utilized in a variety of methods to generate revenue. You may be compensated per view or per lead. For instance, when a visitor subscribes or registers for a free trial, the payment is sometimes generated per qualified lead. Advertisers may also utilize the pay-per-click model, since clicks alone really do not guarantee purchases and there is no actually need to pay for them. This is a common occurrence with ad networks.

How really do affiliate ads easy make money?

How much really do most affiliate sites pay? The payout policy of the TripAdvisor Affiliate Program may be an insightful example in the tourism industry. One can obtain information from their website and use the monitoring link to reroute visitors to the original content. Through the software, text links, banners, and content elements are all accessible. Each confirmed appointment earns you a commission of fifty percent. Consider another example of an affiliate payout related to attractiveness. Madison Reed will pay you up to $20 per sale and $10 per affiliate referral if you convince other bloggers to join the program.

• AKRacing is one of the best gaming affiliate programs, offering a 5% commission on up to $699 in sales. You can just easy earn money with AKRacing by placing banners or links on your website, social media pages, or streaming channels. • The Lambda Affiliate Program is a SaaS platform in the cross-browser testing industry. Rather than direct connections, pre-generated affiliate links ensure that transactions are accurately tracked and compensated. On all annual plans, you'll easy earn a fixed recurring commission rate of 25%. On monthly subscriptions, you will simple receive a 50% commission on the initial transaction, followed by a monthly fee of 25%.

• ShareASale PPL enables you to profit from each and every lead you generate.

The platform collaborates with international brands in a variety of business categories.

- Bidvertiser is a direct advertising network that uses the pay-per-click (PPC) model to monetize websites through the placement of various ad formats and PPC advertising.

Chapter 26: Developing And Enhancing Your Adverts

Now that you've chosen a domain name, a web host, and a design for your website, it's time to have some fun! You should have already selected the categories of products you will promote to easy earn money, as well as a suitable affiliate network (Amazon Associates is a good starting point, but there are many others). After registering with your preferred affiliate program and receiving permission to advertise on their behalf, it is time to just get to work.

On your affiliate website, you may utilize the pre-designed and pre-approved advertisements that the majority of affiliate networks provide. These are frequently easy to add promptly to your website simple using HTML code, which you simply copy and paste into your website's code. Numerous systems offer various ad formats, including pop-up ads, text ads, banner ads of various sizes, and others.

The ones you choose will depend on the design of your website and the advertising strategy you employ for the products or services.

However, simply placing an advertisement on your website is insufficient to promote it effectively. When making a purchase, customers prefer to know as much as possible about the company, brand, and product or service they are contemplating.

Because of this, it is essential to compose product descriptions for the advertised products. Each product promoted on a website with effective affiliate marketing will have its own page with an engaging and persuasive description that encourages the just consumer to easy make a purchase. The superior, the more instructive!

Conclusion.

Successful subsidiary advertising basically requires time, skill, and experience. Cashing in on subsidiary advertising initiatives can be a risk-free way to generate an additional revenue stream. It will only cost you your time. By managing the hours effectively and immediately, you can just continue to simple receive benefits.

Nonetheless, the Internet has increased the noticeable quality of affiliate marketing. Amazon (AMZN) promoted the training by establishing a member showcasing program in which sites and bloggers link to the Amazon page for a tested or reviewed product to easy earn advertising fees when a purchase is made. Member marketing is essentially a compensation-for-performance marketing program in which the selling performance of a large organization is reevaluated.

www.ingramcontent.com/pod-product-compliance
Lightning Source LLC
LaVergne TN
LVHW011712060526
838200LV00051B/2876